Of Lost Things

Of Lost Things

Dani De Luca

Querencia Press, LLC
Chicago Illinois

QUERENCIA PRESS

© Copyright 2024
Dani De Luca

All Rights Reserved

ISBN 978 1 959118 81 7

.

www.querenciapress.com

First Published in 2024

Querencia Press, LLC
Chicago IL

Printed & Bound in the United States of America

Additional Praise

"Dani De Luca's *Of Lost Things* alchemizes what we considered lost, how to mourn about the things we lose, and the different attempts at naming those lost things, be they abstract or concrete. De Luca offers lyric poems that ask you to sit with each line, ask you to feel language as it exists in the speaker's mouth, and to quiet your own conception of a what a poem can do. This collection is a triumph. It weaves the abstraction of mourning through the stories we tell ourselves about our bodies and lives, alongside the many stories we inherit."

—Minadora Macheret, Author of *Love Me, Anyway*

It is such a mysterious place, the land of tears.

—Antoine de Saint-Exupéry

CONTENTS

for the lost and those who seek them

The Noise of Falling

In my country we starve
on purpose. Cram the alchemy
of who we are in size o jeans.
Wear a smile while fainting. Sip
smallness through societal straws.
Wish our pound of flesh was a gram.

We commit to killing ourselves slowly.
Not the bullet but the celery. Not the
high jump but the shallow fade. Ask me
something else. Anything besides how much
my new sins weigh. Place your hand round my
thinning wrist and ask me how empty tastes.

First Mourning

Sometimes words don't come
in a way that's helpful.

Sometimes they come hurting—
an *i* beheaded
a *y* broken to *v*—
and lay upon your pillow,
still warm from your sleeping,
daring for compassion.

You have a choice then
to mend the words
that mourn—
to bright them
and make them
unthem—   or

to write the *i* falling
and the *y* limping
through the pain.

Perhaps that is the kinder thing.

A Kind of Thanksgiving

It is astonishing the pace
at which we're forgotten.
How suddenly we live without
grave speaking loudest.

Such quantum entanglement,
death. Its resonance, miscarried
by young bones. Their minds
a sieve for liquid loss.

Each soul rise and set, watch
how a poet ferries your father
past death and into your
center land. Watch how she

reminds you of his timbre and his
shunting away. Watch how she
watches you watching her, waiting
for words only the splayed of heart hear.

In death, we turn to poets.
They sit beside us. And read.

The Ocean Knows

the ocean knows who you are,
you and your salted lungs
heavy from weeping.

she will untie your hands
and blow gently beneath
trembling wings too heavied to fly.

the ocean knows who you are
you and your words, you must
crawl on hands and knees to find.

she will remind you: *you are not alone*
when warmth is scarce and the ghosts
of those you need don't appear.

the ocean knows who you are
in the middle hours of self, when
hallelujahs have hardened to seeds

of longing that bloom sour. she knows
the grown language of loss—how it
spreads in thin places, making them full.

the ocean knows who you are:
you, medicinal mandrake of mercied
ideas. you, writer of obsessive lists

and delighter in romance. you,
sufferer of occupational heartbreak.
the job is being human.
She knows that too.

In the story she tells

there's a maid, a bathroom, and a crochet hook.

The maid disappears, *as they do*, she says, and is found inside a shade of octopus ink, a bleeding crochet hook wrapped with a trembling hand. Death is everywhere. The dry stones of her teeth click together three times: *There's no place like home,* but she goes nowhere. She is rooted to those marbled tiles, holding what her insides held before. *I'msorryI'msorryI'msosorry,* she says, making her own weather, as bright bolts of *I had to* race down legs once firm on the firma.

In the story she tells, the maid lives, but is never again alive.

Twilight Falls Faster Now

There's a 777 overhead, screaming the skies white,
while our maple undresses below. My husband sits,

tending a fire, and my son races the fence line with
boys yelling *die! die! die!* to unsuspecting fire ants

building and rebuilding. Days fall upon themselves,
pulling their bed sheets neck high and rolling over.

Later we have an ant funeral. My son says a few words
because it's sad to die for being yourself. The air is heavy

with burning wood and youth. I hear the boom of
six-year-old voices splitting the clouds and somewhere,

somehow turning seven. These days origamied
and technicolored crease my face with wonder.

Years from now I'll remember my son and Nora
chalking their hands pink and printing the pavement.

I'll remember the playground's heartbeat and how time
and wind moved him farther from my arms and closer

to the wild wide open of his own.

Before the war

I can bring no more than what I am
into this sliced night. stars fall too fast

for me to catch, brighting the lines
of my face and dewing my lashes.

Oh how this yellow wears me—
its brilliance a skyful of hope,

remembering my shiver of skin
next to yours—knowing your world

was mine
in mine.

we are endlings of grace, roaming the
bright halls of body, traveling heartward

and pausing there. there is no pulse
in which to love. our truth dissolves

in heaving chests and throat swallows.
our welkined sugars divine and fast falling.

Sin-Eater

I wonder why we die on unnecessary
hills and swallow stones formed by

others. I looked into my horse's mouth
once and saw the watermelon snow

of the Himalayas and its ghosts of
blueberries and chives. There was a

man in the shadows, standing over a
prone female body, unmoving.

I watched him reach down and eat the
bread placed on her chest by those who

loved her. And saw him
stumble from the weight of it.

Who knows how many sins he had eaten
before he laid upon the pink cold and became it.

Freshmen

I met you in your tarnished temple,
a sliver of person so delicate
you nearly took to the wind
by breathing.

You were a poet, a lover of love
(and French and cigarettes) and boys
pretending, somewhat convincingly,
to be men.

I saw one leave your room once
and wondered if he filled you
with anything more than
his empty seed.

Later, you read to me
from *The Little Prince*:

On ne voit bien qu'avec le coeur,
l'essentiel est invisible pour les yeux.
It is only with the heart that one can see rightly;
what is essential is invisible to the eye.

You continued on, without the page in
front of you, staring past the landscape of me.
I didn't understand the words then
but now I know you were saying:

I am in a falling year.
Please, please, don't catch me.

The Hatchlings

Look, I can float, he says,
tipping his body forward,

smiling. In these moments,
he isn't alone and doesn't

miss the siblings he knows
I held but didn't birth living.

In the quiet moments, he
tells me he's glad he grew

where they tried to, but
couldn't. *We all know*

your insides, mama, but
only I know your outsides.

I wonder if I stepped in front
of a light, you'd see them through

my paper skin, still torn by loss
after loss after loss after loss.

And wonder who I'd be as a mother
of five instead of a mother of

"only one". *There's still time,*
they say. *Why not try again?*

they say. *How sad it's only him,*
they say. In the pool, he sits on

an imaginary nest, beaming.
Look, Mama, four eggs!

After a successful hatching, I
watch him place imaginary

worms in their imaginary mouths,
then whisper, *I love you, brothers.*

I love you, sister. I don't have to
imagine what kind of brother he'd
be. I watch him feed his siblings and
know.

Grief Haibun

Grief rearranges us. As children, it fuses bones on impact: bones that need time to expand from 300 to 206 do not have it. They grow so large the skin screams through sewn lips, holding taut the beating death of *forgotten, left behind, Survivor.* As adults, grief shrinks those same bones, collapsing heart and lungs in a coffin of ribs and sternum. The linen of skin hangs, creased in new places that can't unlose loss; and you are smaller, somehow, in the big of it.

Grief rearranges.

If you don't yet know it, friend,

hand to heart, you will.

March 5, 2022

My son started speaking in *should*. I shouldn't be surprised,
should I?
We all do—speak in *should*, I mean.

He is six today and asks about his birthday cake and play date
and the
strollers parked at the Przemyśl station, waiting.

I should tell him of the non-simple solid of love, I know. Of
women who,
like the dignified peach, bruise delicious. Women whose bodies
know war
has no end when it lives within.

I pull him to me, cradle him as I did when he met my outsides
for the first
time. I should tell him of love, I know. But like the women of
Poland,
I show him instead.

Details

A Scottish Seer
told me to look
for the dead in
the details.

It is not the plane,
but the wrecked wing,
not the angel,
but its hazeled hem.

We are surrounded
by living dead,
still beating and
breathing.

And yes they are
in everything, but
slip in the specific
to the far-from
near of them.

It is important to feel
the loss of loss and know
your father in the split breast
of sparrow and the Prussian blue
of near night.

And when it pours, listen
for the tiny halos of fallen
angels hurled against your
panes.

The dead
(our dead)
are there, too.

Poem Beginning with a Line from Smith

> *Every truth you tell is a kindness, even if it*
> *makes people uncomfortable. And every truth you don't*
> *tell is an unkindness, even if it makes people comfortable.*
>
> —*Glennon Doyle*

My son is sprawled on his back, arms flung don't- shoot wide,
sleeping.
He is six and safe. He doesn't know New York or its gutting
news.

Doesn't know the atrocities of humans or hunting or humans
hunting humans. Doesn't know that skin color can be (and so
often is)

a death sentence. Doesn't know white boys like him plan and
prep and
pepper social media with what they're gun(na) do before they
do it and

what happens after it happens. And by *it*, I mean murder. Dead
black
bodies—ten, *this time*—bleeding the ground red in Buffalo.
Bleeding

the ground red, everywhere. Bodies that should be warm and whole

and *here*. Bodies that should be sleeping. Like my son. Only sleeping.

Bitter

Sugar does not sweeten everything.
Pour it over a limb, dangling; a corpse,
still warm; a child, violated.

It will not sweeten what cannot be,
what must be bitter for full moon after
full moon, until you call it new.

Soaring Stars

At 34,000 feet you cannot see the 18-year-old, his AR-15

or the stardust of fourth graders floating upward. The air

is thin here. But not the outrage. That is thick like the night

we fly through. I avoid the window, dodging the constellations

of children hanging from the inked tulle. My son leans over—

same age as those of Sandy Hook but younger than those of
Robb—

*What happens when you get shot, Mama? Does your heart stop
beating?*

Sometimes, I say, *but not always.* I watch him sit with the
sometimes.

I want to tell him there won't be others. That guns will make us

safer, despite being outnumbered by them. That I won't hold
my

breath watching him walk through his school's front doors. But

I won't lie to him or tell him to pray. Clearly, no one is listening.

I watch stars zoom across the darkened dark.

I will not call them *shooting.*

The 18-year-old did that. Shot stars.

From now on, I will call them *soaring*.

Small Roads

Take the small roads—
the ones through, not around.

Drive past the high school, the grocery
store, the funeral home/furniture store.

Stand on the strip of grass separating me
from you. Notice how it's less green there.

Even lifeless. Grab a coffee or tea and sit
where we used to. Watch as our memories

walk in and out of places our cells stayed.
Touch your cheek. Feel my breath there still.

Mother-in-Law's Tongue

In autumn she ran away
with vagabonds and learned
to swallow fire and eat glass
in ways different from home.

When night felled its ink
above the folded world of her legs,
she ran her fingers over their
scarred-by-thrown-knives topography,
remembering.

She hadn't sat close to despair.
She hadn't held its hand saying
I know, damn you. Instead she led
a squad of siblings up and down
impossible hills, eyes closed and
arms wide open.

She set tires alight and disappeared
cats and dreams in the river, awaiting
her father's drunken arrival,
rehearsing ways to be invisible.

She practiced being the more
they demanded
and yoked herself
to the less she believed.

It is no wonder the circus called to her.
Their more was art and patchwork tents
and conversations that included the words
I and *we.*

Her parents are gone now,
yet I find her open mouthed
over the flames of them.
Some things, I've learned,
cannot be extinguished.

For Liza

In the suburban jungle, women
are hunted for sport.

They leave to run errands or
simply run and

are dragged to black SUV's—
painted with pleas and screams—

where their scarlet life force
is diluted with floor cleaner.

One cannot make this shit up.
How women's voices, raised

in supplication, open the mouth
of the whole damn sky.

i was taught to be prey

i was taught to pretty and please
and polite and pardon the predator.
i was taught to run, but not fast.
to speak, but not loud. to blend

and hide and fold myself so as not

to find myself. i was taught to fear

god and ignore goddess.

i was taught the force of flesh.

prey and pray, separated by one letter

and a chasm of meaning. when i was

preyed upon, i prayed.

you know what i prayed for?

forgiveness.

i have stopped praying that prayer.

Maybe Wind Is Not What They Told Us

I wonder where unscreamed screams of women go.
Do they twist around intestine and colon, sealing the
waste of you within you—the waste then wasting you raw?

Do they sink to gut and populate the tissue there?
Making it glow inflamed? Making its future inhabitants glow
too?

Do they ribbon pharynx, jaw, lips, and tongue, then pull
tightly, closing what open allows?

Or do cells of unscreamed screams travel our exhales, joining
millions of their furied sisters to blow leaves from trees and rip
roofs from houses and send 1,700 pounds of water toward sleepy
marine villages?

Maybe wind is not what they told us. Maybe wind has nothing
to do with the high pressure of atmosphere and everything to
do

with the high pressure of gentle women, violated (in every way
one can be),
since the beginning's beginning.

Maybe wind is our reckoning—
our unscreamed screams
matched and married for battle.

Of Lost Things

My greatest job as mother
is to teach my child to lose.

Lose at soccer and Uno.
Lose his gifted crucifix
(maybe pray to Saint Anthony,
maybe not).

Lose a battle   a tooth   a friend
            (who never was a friend
                or was the very best).

Lose illusion   expectation
self-and-othered oppression.
Lose a beta fish by over /
                / under feeding.

Lose the idea that accumulation of
people + plenty + power =
Purpose.
Lose the idea that dispersion of
people + plenty + power =
Irrelevance.

Lose the idea that his humanity is
different than mine   (or yours).
Lose the idea that   war is far
and   man is free
and   life is fair.

Lose the idea of not losing me.

I will teach him to lose me

and how to go on when he loses self-
                        confidence
                      motivation
                            worth
          (it happens to us all).

I will teach my child to lose
and perhaps
when loss comes
he will remember.

After Another Death, My Son Asks About Mine & Where to Find Me

This star rise,
laundry calls.

Low and long vowels
travel the hallways

and find me, reading.

This is my piece of sky
to hold, then fold neatly—

my heart quantum
pressed into its fabric.

My scent in the stitches.
My voice in each seam.

I am in every hung and
folded item. The beloved

and once loved. The items
too small for him now

that I remove, fold again,
but keep, while crying.

A pink shirt slides over
his slim trunk and lays

over his heart, beating.
There is nectar in this

nounless work of being.
There is nectar in the

clean sound of a shirt
hitting the floor at day's

end. And my being there.
Still.

Acknowledgments

– The epigraph is from Antoine de Saint-Exupéry, *The Little Prince* © Antoine de Saint-Exupéry Estate

– The epigraph in "Poem Beginning with a Line from Smith" is from Glennon Doyle, *Untamed* © Glennon Doyle & Dial Press

Thanks

Loving thanks to Renato and Massimo for chasing me through the depths of my own heart.

Loving thanks to Brooke—best friend, reader and divine human. You teach me daily.

Loving thanks to those in the ALLOW writing space. Thank you for showing up and bleeding.

Loving thanks to Querencia Press, especially Emily and Vee, for seeing me.

Loving thanks to those who applauded or disapproved. Both buoyed.

And, finally, loving thanks to my father, who believed.

Milton Keynes UK
Ingram Content Group UK Ltd.
UKHW021909020524
442050UK00014B/546

9 781959 118817